OFFICIAL Donovan 1990

£3.99

Published in Great Britain by World International Publishing Limited.
An Egmont Company, P.O. Box 111, Great Ducie Street,
Manchester M60 3BL.
Printed in Great Britain.
ISBN 7235 6866-9
1st Reprint 1989

Contents

Design: Visible Ink Pty Ltd.
                Don Barbuto
                Michael Fettes
                Philip Philippou

Words: Glen Blackmore

Typesetting: Bandaid Productions Pty Ltd

Photography: Lawrence Lawry
                Peter Mac
                Serge Thomann
                Tim Bauer
                Dayved Jones

Management: Richard East

*Production
Co-ordinator:*   Noleine Blizzard

Jason would like to thank
Terry Donovan, Heather 'Lips' Nette,
Sharon McPhilemy (PWL), Georgina Howe
(ABC Television), Kerry Theobold and Brian Walsh
(Network 10 Australia), Sue Foster (Sharp End
Promotions), The Mighty Music Machine.

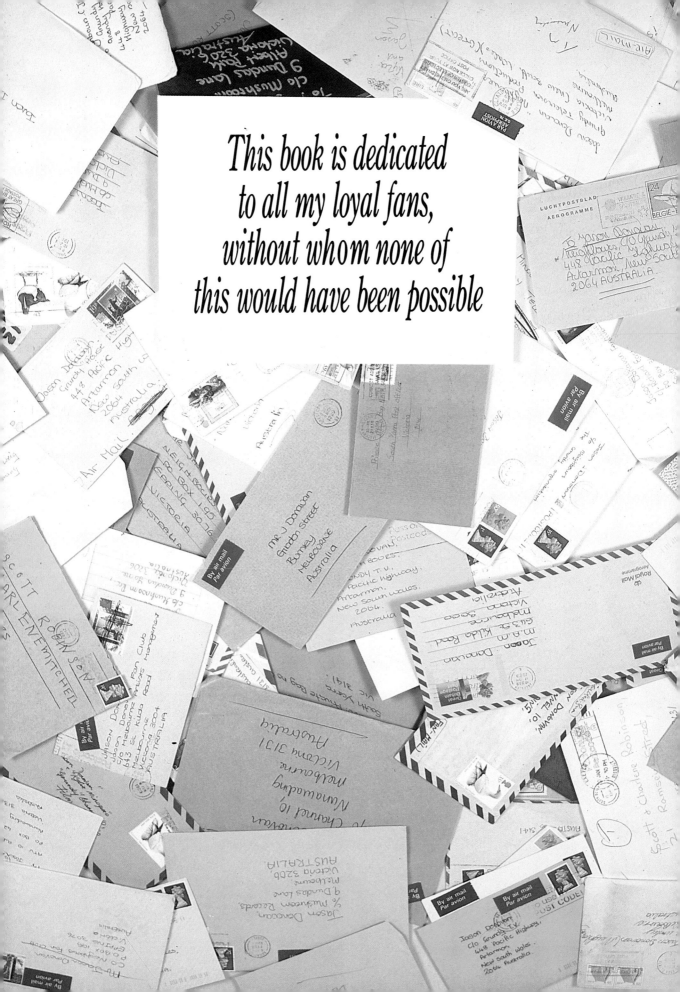

*This book is dedicated
to all my loyal fans,
without whom none of
this would have been possible*

A Letter from Jason

Dear Reader

1988 was such a great year, but I have to say that 1989 is shaping up to be incredible; new singles, a mini-series, an album and possibly a film. For me, the highlight would have to be my first album "Ten Good Reasons", which is a personal landmark and I hope you enjoy it as much as I did making it.

This year also gives me a chance to visit many new countries which is something I am really looking forward to. I love to travel and to have the opportunity to meet new people.

I'm also very happy that I've had the chance to finish this annual (at last!) and I hope you like it as much as I've enjoyed working on it.

I've included many photos you will not have seen before and I hope I've managed to give you an insight into my day to day life as well as feature the many special moments of the year.

Thanks for the support and encouragement you have given over the past year; it makes the hard work worthwhile.

I really hope you enjoy the annual. See you soon.

Jason Donovan

The Story So Far . . .

"I don't think I ever stopped to think about it," says Jason. Opportunities and success just keep on coming, but Jason is not just an overnight star. For most of his life, he has been a part of the entertainment industry, learning the ins and outs as he grew up.

On June 1st 1968, Jason Sean was born into a show business family. His father, Terence Donovan, was a stage and screen actor with credits in England and Australia. His mother, Susan, was a well known presenter for a children's show in Australia called "Adventure Island".

Even after his parents divorced, and Jason went to live with his father, he was never far from the stage.

From his early years at the quaint Malvern Central School, Jason developed habits of

learning and observation that would unknowingly set him on his path to stardom. "My Dad was in DIVISION 4" (a top rating local police show in the early seventies) and, Jason remembers, "I would go from school and hang around the set."

For Jason, this wasn't anything special. Like most boys that age, he was obsessed with aircraft. His ambition then was to be a pilot.

By the time he began secondary school at De La Salle College in Melbourne, Jason had developed a very close bond with his father. Curiosity and a sense of fun prompted

him to persuade his father to allow him to try out for bit parts in television. "The first time I stood in front of a camera was for a SKYWAYS episode. I was nervous. I still do get quite nervous about learning lines. But as a kid, it was fun, I didn't have much work." Small parts in two episodes were fitted in between school, piano lessons and singing with the Australian Boys Choir.

The next year, at the age of 12, he was in another television series called "I CAN JUMP PUDDLES". This was followed a year later by a role in HOME, another series. He continued to follow his father's career on the stage with little thought of joining him. For Jason, it was just a bit of fun, and he continued on with school, the piano and singing. His father encouraged a level headed approach to life and advised him to finish school.

In his final year of school, Jason was still unsure of his future. "I never planned to become an actor because I always thought it was such an insecure profession. But the thought of an apprenticeship was boring." In 1984 he went to another audition, for a new show called NEIGHBOURS.

"I wasn't counting on getting the part so I sort of relaxed into it," recalls Jason. "They came back to me and said the part's yours, how do you feel about it? I knew I would have to give up school, I was a bit wary about that. I didn't know what to do. My father said forget it, there would be plenty of other opportunities. But I went to the school and talked to the headmasters. They said it was an opportunity of a lifetime."

Despite his teacher's advice to leave school and pursue the part, Jason decided to reject the role. In the end, he was right.

The show was a flop. Six months later, a revamped NEIGHBOURS was bought by another television network. "It was destiny I suppose, I got the part back when it resumed

production at Channel Ten." Within months, Jason was making his mark in the industry.

In 1987, he won a "Logie", Australian television's equivalent of the Emmys, for "Best New Talent". This was rapidly followed by a "Best Actor" commendation from the Australian Television Society.

From there, success just steamrolled for the "kid from Ramsay St.". In March, 1988, he won the "Logie" for "Most

Popular Actor" for his role as Scott Robinson. That same month Jason signed a recording contract with Mushroom

Records. This was also a logical extension of his talents, after all he had completed three years with a national choir and five years of piano. Even so, it wasn't until he met Pete Waterman some months later that Jason found the musical style that suited him.

His first trip to London in April was for NEIGHBOURS. "I was amazed. I don't think anybody back in Australia can conceive how big the show is here. I was just so grateful to have the show work quite well in Australia. Then we topped the ratings, and the show went overseas. The response was incredible."

In July, he recorded his first single "Nothing can divide us" for producers Stock, Aitken, Waterman. Released first in Great Britain, it reached number 4 in August. Jason's reaction to all this? Typically level headed and modest. "As a kid, I would watch "Countdown", "Top of the Pops", and those sort of shows, and watch all those English recording artists. It's sort of weird, suddenly, I've become one myself."

Back in Australia, Jason began filming in "THE HEROES", a mini-series based on the real life exploits of a group of commandos. "Nothing can divide us" is released in early October and reaches number 5. In between all his acting commitments, he finds time to do a duet with Kylie Minogue.

In December, 1988, "Especially for you" is released internationally and is a number one hit in six countries. At home, it reaches number two. Jason was thrilled; it had proved that his success was not solely based on NEIGHBOURS. It was a huge

success in countries that had never seen the television show.

Jason's third single, "Too many broken hearts" was released in England in March 1989. It reached number one in its second week. He is now a star. "My determination was to make it number one, and it has ... it's fantastic. I never thought when I was at school that I would hold Madonna off the number one spot. But it doesn't change life, you still go on, I'm still the same. You've just got to keep your feet on the ground." Public appearances remind older people of the Beatles days. He is constantly before the people on television, in the press, and on the radio. In April, his first and eagerly awaited album is released.

Jason Donovan is a household word, but fame has not gone to his head. His smile is genuine. He loves his work and his fans. Most importantly, there is a lot more to come. Good on you, mate. Here's to the future...

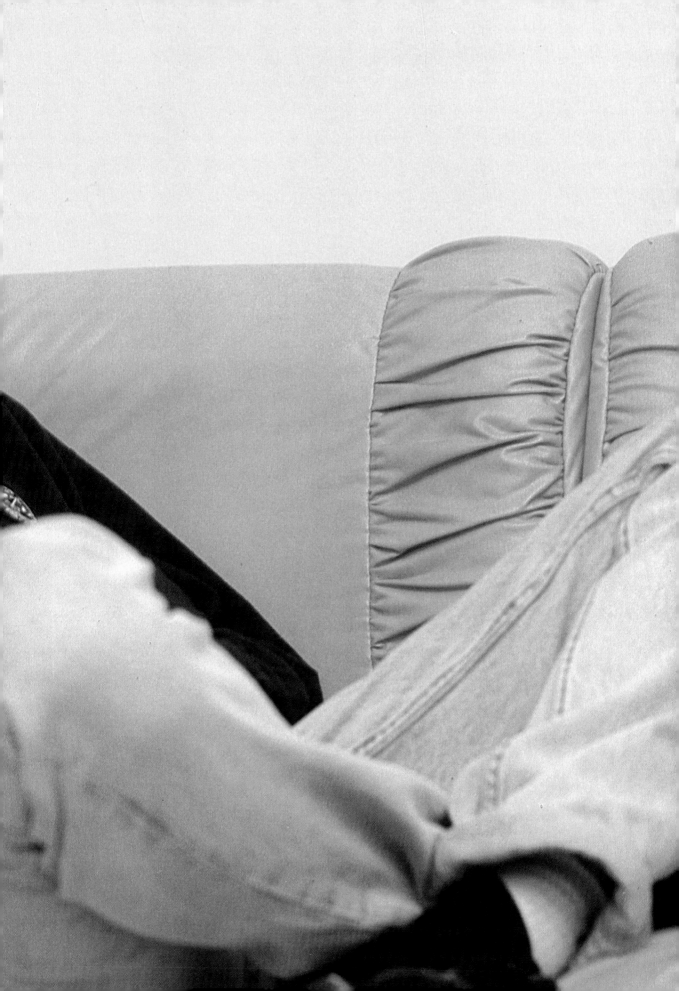

5.30am-6.00am

Jason gets out of bed very early in order to prepare for the long day ahead.
Usually he has a good breakfast while he goes over his schedule for the day.
He always starts the day with a few glasses of freshly squeezed juice.
Sometimes he re-reads the scenes for Neighbours which he has studied the night before.

6.45am

Jason heads off on a vigorous run early in the morning. He likes to keep very fit as it helps him cope with the long hours he has to endure.

8.00am-9.00am

After the run, it's time to get ready for work. Jason needs to check in at his manager's office every day.
Here, he may do a few interviews over the telephone as there is never enough time to meet with each journalist personally.
There are also many business matters which need to be attended to and Jason likes to keep informed of everything on a daily basis.

9.15am-7.00pm

Now it's time to drive out to the Channel 10 studios for a day on the "Neighbours" set. It usually takes Jason around 20 minutes to drive to the television station and on arrival he checks in at the Wardrobe and Make-up department to make the change to "Scott Robinson".
Each scene is rehearsed prior to recording. The actors spend a great deal of time making sure that their lines and movements are correct, prior to the cameras recording the scenes.

By the time the cameras are ready to roll, everyone knows exactly what they have to do.

It is not unusual for 10 scenes to be recorded on one day and they are not always for the same episode of "Neighbours". Jason may record 2 or 3 scenes for one episode and then make wardrobe changes in order to perform in other scenes which may be recorded for episodes 1 or 2 weeks later . . . it can get a little confusing!

Once Jason is at the studio he usually has to stay the whole day, even though there might be some free time between scenes. He usually learns lines or does other business in this free time and then takes a few mintues to get some lunch. After lunch he continues with his scenes until the schedule is completed.

7.15pm

Jason leaves the studio and heads for home. On his way home he stops off for a brief swim at the beach. Jason tries to swim every day, regardless of the temperature!

8.15pm

After a 30 minute swim, Jason makes his way home to get ready for dinner. Sometimes he will stay at home and prepare his own meal but often he ventures out to one of his favourite restaurants in Melbourne.

9.15pm

Time to go home and learn his lines for tomorrow's scenes. Depending on the number of scenes being recorded, Jason will spend 2 or 3 hours learning his lines before going to bed. He sometimes watches a little bit of television, or listens to music, to relax before going to bed.

JASON *by the* ST★RS

GEMINI
May 21st to June 21st

Geminis are friendly and concerned for others. They love to spend time with friends. Many "twins" are inspired to right wrongs. An Air type, Geminis are concerned with all types of communication. As a result they tend towards acting and politics.

Geminis like to live well. Theirs is a world of movement, they hate being tied down and dislike all forms of drudgery or monotony. The Gemini is a restless spirit, liable to think the grass is greener elsewhere.

They refuse to let emotion confuse their thinking, but their quick wittedness and charm easily impresses others. They tend to conceal their inner feelings and their two-sided nature can make them puzzling partners.

They are generally vivacious persons who have a need to make life vital and beautiful for themselves.

CHINESE HOROSCOPE

The Chinese year begins on February 6. 1989 is the year of the Snake, a year when hard work and dedication will be rewarded.

Birth year sign
MONKEY

The monkey will go far in 1989 but success will depend on attitude and determination. The Monkey should not become too complacent. This is a year when the Monkey must not take undue risks.

This year will be active socially and the Monkey will charm and impress many with his wit. Personal relationships should be treated with great care; this year, the Monkey should be careful with criticism.

At some stage during the year, there will be considerable pressure, and although eager to please, the Monkey must protect his health by occasionally putting himself first. A few short breaks will be most beneficial.

The year of the snake will look kindly upon enterprises, and financial matters should go well. The Monkey, with his naturally inquisitive mind, is likely to explore some fascinating new interests in 1989.

15

STROLLING THROUGH

RAMSAY ST.

There are quite a few surprises for anyone who turns up to watch NEIGHBOURS in production. One is the size of the production area at Channel Ten. Working your way through the security and reception areas, you navigate a rabbit warren of offices to emerge into something like a huge aircraft hangar.

At one end are the various interior sets: offices, lounge rooms, kitchens, and other rooms that are occupied by the various characters of the show. Some areas are in semi-darkness, cluttered with props and it is difficult to identify them. Overhead, a constellation of powerful lights dangle, ready to light each in turn.

The set is like a crazy fun palace; doors that lead nowhere, walls that move, gardens that turn out to be narrow alleyways between plywood walls. Each room appears fully enclosed, but one wall is missing to allow the cameras in.

In the middle of the production area is a props bay the size of a small football field. Around this area is the carpentry section, make-up, cafeteria and a loose grouping of offices.

The other surprise is not finding people running around in a panic, nerves raw with pressure. In fact, the NEIGHBOURS set is amazingly calm, especially for a show that rates so well and involves so many people. Of course there is pressure, but everyone seems to take it well.

The public address system booms occasionally, summoning people here and there, but cast and crew smile and joke in between takes. But things can, and do, go wrong. The occasional bomb scare or power glitch can create mayhem. Then the pressure is doubled to meet the schedule.

Nearly half the shooting is done on location. This generally means out the

for a close-up, and everything is ready for a take. There is no set number of takes to get a scene right. Sometimes it is done in one, other times three or four. Back stage, quiet conversations stop dead, silence. The scene is done in one take. Actors move off to be replaced by others in a different set.

Jason is relaxed, pleased that this one went so easily. He heads for Wardrobe and changes clothes, ready

"survival" — here, they can relax and unwind a little when time allows.

The director reschedules some scenes. Suddenly a two hour break is now only twenty minutes. Jason's scene has moved forward. An additional scene is required. There's no complaint, this sort of thing happens. For Jason, the adrenalin pumps again, he gets ready to slip back into the character of Scott.

The Cast of Neighbours

back of Channel Ten itself or in the suburban street a few blocks away that shares the same name.

In the actual Ramsay St. scenes are kept to a minimum to avoid disrupting the lives of the residents too much. But there is no shortage of other residents and councils who offer their streets as locations.

It might seem glamorous for the actual residents of Ramsay St. but it does have its drawbacks. Painting or landscaping has to be worked into the script so that there is continuity. Can't have a house changing colour overnight can we?

Back on the set, Jason is going through a rehearsal. For this scene, it goes smoothly; minor changes of movement, repositioning a typewriter

for the next scene. Make-up is checked but not altered. All of the actors wear make-up for the whole day. It's very necessary for maintaining a natural look under the bright television lights. For Jason, it is an extra job; his sensitive skin requires special cleansers to remove it. He does this each evening at home.

In between his calls, he spends the time in a variety of ways; learning lines, making phone calls, discussing performances with other actors, grabbing a bite to eat. It's a long day, none of it is wasted. Twelve hour days are not unusual.

At one side of the studio is the Green room. This is the actors' lounge. While all the actors keep surprisingly busy, this room is essential for their

Despite the long day, the smile is ever ready, he flashes his apology and leaves for the set. It is exhausting just watching all this. Being an actor, let alone a star, is long, hard work.

BEHIND THE SCENES OF NEIGHBOURS

SUCCESS MEETS SUCCESS

Stock, Aitken, Waterman are probably the most successful songwriters and producers of the decade. In four years they produced an incredible 48 hits. "As soon as we came together we took off," says Mike, the team's major songwriter. "When we started we had nothing but a dream." The trio have worked extremely hard and their success is the result of listening to the public. It was the fans that led them to Jason.

"The first time I met Pete Waterman was at the Old Kent Road studios, before they burnt down. He came into the studio while I was recording some demos. The initial contact was between Mushroom Records and Pete; they had distribution links with acts like Kylie and Bananarama."

"Mushroom Records originally signed me up. I tried a NOISEWORKS song first, entitled 'Reach Out'. It was a good song but didn't really suit me. Pete Waterman suggested a different style and you can't argue with someone who's been in the business for such a long time and can predict what can happen.

"Pete Waterman is the businessman; he runs PWL, the record label that Stock, Aitken, Waterman songs go out on. He is responsible for bringing it all together.

"Mike Stock is the main writer; he forms the ideas, goes through the lyrics with you. Matt Aitken is a great guitar player and he contributes to the writing of songs as well. I recorded "Especially for you" with Matt because Mike didn't fly out to Australia at that time. In a way that was quite unusual. Mike also plays keyboards. As a team they work very well."

Stock, Aitken, Waterman have a unique way of working, and a unique attitude. They listen to the public. The critics might want to analyse, but basically it's the public who decide what they want to listen to. This trio have proved that point.

"The good thing about the building they work in is that everything is done in the one place; recording, promotion, distribution. It creates a really good atmosphere, and gets people motivated."

The final word about this partnership is best summed up in a comment Jason made after hearing their work: "The best thing about the music they produce is that it's positive. It makes you feel good."

STOCK ● AITKEN ● WATERMAN

JASON DONOVAN

NOTHING CAN DIVIDE US

"Nothin

"Because it was the first song, I was a bit nervous. Like anything new, it took a while to grasp what was required.

"It was written a bit high and I wanted everything to work. But I managed and it was a lot of fun. I was amazed at the reaction when it was released. It launched my singing career and in that way I'm very grateful.

"It is a good song and at the time I was very enthusiastic about it. Taken for what it is, it's fine. I've got used to the style of Stock, Aitken, Waterman since, and that's made a difference.

"The video was different. When I first saw it, I quite enjoyed it, but looking back on it I would have liked the opportunity to make suggestions and changes. We're actually reshooting some of it for a compilation video to be released later this year."

THE VIDEO

Produced by: Tantamount Productions

Directed by: Rob Wellington

Locations: Metro Nightclub and various locations around Melbourne, Australia

g can divide us''

OR·YOU

"This song was recorded over one night. Matt Aitken and Pete Waterman flew out from London to Australia and we put down the tracks for an A and B side. It was done at Rhinoceros Studios in Sydney.

"Kylie and I didn't actually sing together on it. We did our parts separately.

"I did have some reservations at first, but Kylie and I discussed it. We decided that if it worked in countries other than Australia and Britain, we would have achieved something with the critics."

The single certainly achieved that. It charted well in countries that had never heard or seen them before. It proved that there was more to their talent than the publicity from NEIGHBOURS could give them.

"I was doing "THE HEROES" at the time so I had to juggle that and the video. We did it in Sydney. It was shot over a period of a week. The song's great and we tried to portray a romance through the video in such a way as to keep people wondering."

THE VIDEO
Produced by: *Short Stories*
Directed by: *Chris Langman*
Location: *Various locations around Sydney*

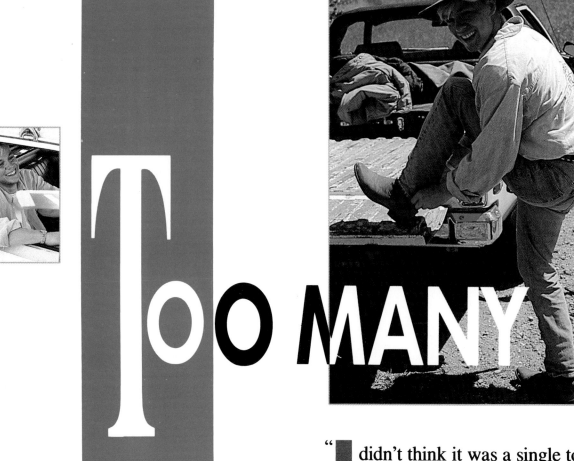

TOO MANY

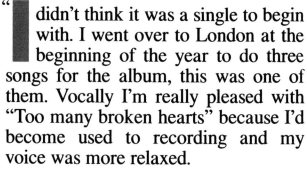

"I didn't think it was a single to begin with. I went over to London at the beginning of the year to do three songs for the album, this was one of them. Vocally I'm really pleased with "Too many broken hearts" because I'd become used to recording and my voice was more relaxed.

"It's one of my favourite songs now.

"We did the video at a place called Falls Creek which is about four hours drive from Melbourne. It was shot in two days including redoing a few shots I wasn't particularly happy with. I was very pleased with the photography.

"My manager, Richard, rang me at six in the morning and said you're number one. It was a wild, strange feeling."

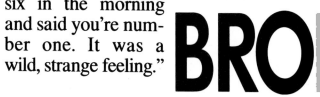

-N HEARTS

THE VIDEO
Produced by: *Short Stories*
Directed by: *Chris Langman*
Location: *Mount Beauty,*
Victoria

CHART SUCCESS AROUND THE WORLD

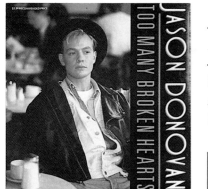

Chart positions available at time of printing

Fitting the interview into the hectic schedule that surrounded Jason's final weeks with NEIGHBOURS wasn't easy. We spoke inbetween rehearsals and scenes, his easy going manner and infectious smile hid the pressure.

What's a typical day like for you while you're doing NEIGHBOURS?

"Today is pretty typical. I started at eight. Last night I got home at nine. Usually it takes an hour, hour and a half to learn the dialogue for the next day. Of course, that depends on how much you are involved on that day. Sometimes, you may only have a few words in a scene, so you don't have to spend hours learning it. When I get up I go for a run or a swim to put me in a good frame of mind. Then I come in, get made up, find wardrobe, rehearse, do my scenes. Usually you have breaks because you don't always have ten scenes in a row. It's all shot out of sequence, so you never have the consistency of knowing what's coming up next."

How do you unwind after a day like that?

"I sit at home, play music. Lately there's been other work. I go to Richard's (Richard East, his manager) office and sort out work there. Then grab a bit to eat, or go out to dinner. It depends on what's coming up the next day. If it's a big day I have to take it a lot easier."

After three and a half years of being "Scott", do you still find him an interesting character?

"Sure. He's become a lot more interesting. The last few story lines have become quite strong. There was a lot of challenge when Kylie was here; it was interesting to work closely with a female, I enjoyed that. Everyone thought that the challenge would not be as great when she left. But it has made me push myself more. Scott has become stronger, much more level-headed. I think I've improved as an actor much more too, so I've been able to put more into the role. He hasn't changed, only got better I think. That's why I'm leaving, he's reached a pinnacle so to speak."

What's next in terms of acting?

"There's a strong possibility of a movie in August, September."

Apart from that?

"I'm going overseas to promote the album. I come back for my twenty-first. I'll be doing a lot of television appearances, radio work . . ."

— *we are interrupted by a loudspeaker paging system. Various people are summoned for rehearsals and scenes. It is obvious that part of Jason is constantly alert for his summons. People seem to be constantly on the move here.*

You seem so relaxed in all your television interviews. . .

"I think what it is . . . I'm so used to having a camera pointing at me. Some people might say I'm blasé about it, but that's not it. For me, it's great, the more used to it I get, the more natural I'll be in performances, interviews, anything. I still get nervous but it depends on the interviewer."

What's been the most difficult interview so far?

"I've had a lot of interviews that tried to tackle certain issues with me. Especially certain journalists. I think it's a challenge, I enjoy it. I enjoy the situation where a journalist is intent on getting something out of me. It's exciting to be able to sit there and play the game the way they're playing it. I've had so much thrown at me over the last three years, I've learned a lot. It's like a tennis match."

 **with** *Jason*

I know you work hard at not letting it change you, but how do you feel about the success that you've encountered?

"I'm excited about it. The one thing that's more exciting than anything is, at the age of twenty I've found what I really want to do with my life. It's been a lot of luck, and a lot of hard work, but I don't have to search anymore. A lot of people my age don't know what they want to

opening night. I'm not into that stuff. I live in a small place . . . my life's changed . . . but I've missed things too. Someone else my age can jump in a car and go wherever, and just surf for a year. I've had to be willing to learn, to sacrifice a few things."

Does success bother you in any way?

"It means I can't go out to a club sometimes and just hang out, mix with the crowd. When I went to

see *Jason. They've been allowed in, and the walk, several hundred metres through office areas and sets, has increased their anxiety. Jason is introduced to them and his face beams genuine pleasure whilst signing their books. After a minute or two they leave and he sits down again.*

How do you feel about all your fans?

"I feel overawed sometimes. In a way I don't understand it. It's stag-

> **❝It's staggering to think when I walk into the studio that some thirty million people will watch. I'm indebted to my fans. I remember how I got started; it's those kids there, they're the ones who count. ❞**

do, and have to find themselves, where they're going. I'm really lucky, I've found it. But the minute I think I know it all, I know it will be time to walk away. Success itself doesn't worry me so long as I'm enjoying what I'm doing. Some people think all acting is, is getting on the front pages and looking great. It's not, it's dedication."

Has it changed you despite your efforts?

"Success is not that the whole world becomes perfect. It doesn't. I live well but . . . I don't travel around in limousines, go to every

New York, I just had the best time. Sounds silly, but it was like the only place to go to get peace and quiet. I was a nobody there. As much as I enjoy success, and I wouldn't want to give anything up, it was great to do anything I wanted. I didn't have to worry about photographers leaping out. Sounds bizarre. I went on one holiday, and the photos turned up on front pages. Sometimes you become so public, there are times you need to think about yourself."

— *At that point we are interrupted by some teenage fans who have been waiting patiently at the security gate to*

gering to think when I walk into the studio that some thirty million people will watch. I'm indebted to my fans. I remember how I got started; it's those kids there, they're the ones who count. It doesn't matter so much about Mr. So and So from the SUN HERALD or the DAILY MIRROR, the fans made me. You've got to be loyal to them."

— *Jason's call comes. He moves onto the set comfortably, the change to Scott almost instantaneous. The energy is there, after all this time he still projects assurance and pleasure in the work. The performance is smooth.*

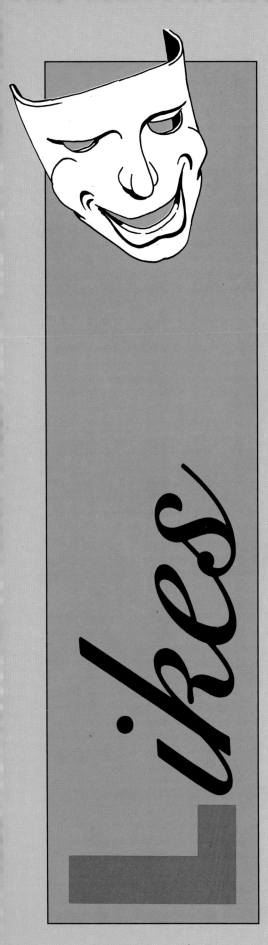

Likes

"**I** guess the best thing is being around friends, and being around people who accept me for being me."

"**I** like quiet, mysterious women; ones that are enthusiastic about life."

"**I** like to get in a car and go down the coast." Jason likes to get away from it all; he loves to surf at the beach resorts south west of Melbourne — Torquay, Apollo Bay, Anglesea and Lorne.

Playing keyboards or guitar "along to tracks I listen to at home. With music you can be yourself."

"**I** love light, sunny environments." One of Jason's loves is his house. There, he is able to satisfy his artistic abilities with remodelling, decorating and painting. He describes it as "nothing flash", but it obviously means a great deal in helping him relax and deal with the pressures of work.

He likes to go out to nightclubs, parties and dinner with friends. He finds he has less time for that now.

Jason also enjoys seeing his family as much as he can. "You work at such a frantic pace that you really need that normality to keep you down to earth."

Keeping fit is one of his passions. Jason runs every day, and swims as often as he can.

"**I** love art and painting." In his final year of school, before NEIGHBOURS came along, Jason was considering a career as a graphic artist in an advertising agency. He says now, "I don't know that I'd find it so interesting now, I've found the direction I want to head in."

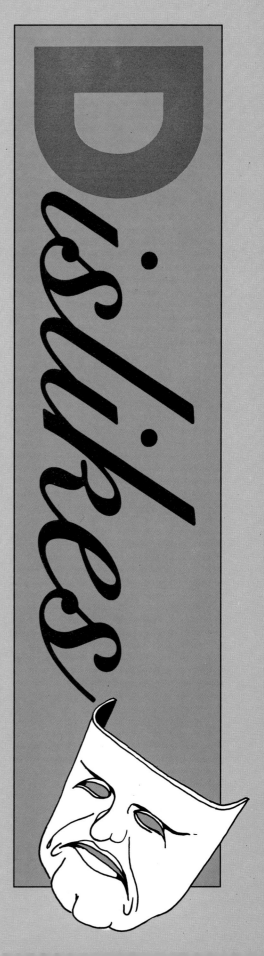

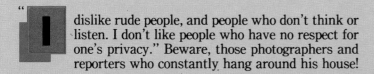 dislike rude people, and people who don't think or listen. I don't like people who have no respect for one's privacy." Beware, those photographers and reporters who constantly hang around his house!

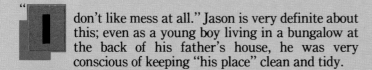 don't like mess at all." Jason is very definite about this; even as a young boy living in a bungalow at the back of his father's house, he was very conscious of keeping "his place" clean and tidy.

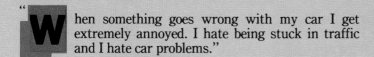 hen something goes wrong with my car I get extremely annoyed. I hate being stuck in traffic and I hate car problems."

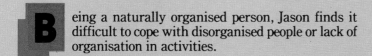 eing a naturally organised person, Jason finds it difficult to cope with disorganised people or lack of organisation in activities.

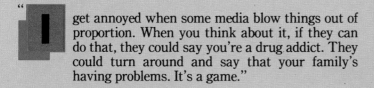 get annoyed when some media blow things out of proportion. When you think about it, if they can do that, they could say you're a drug addict. They could turn around and say that your family's having problems. It's a game."

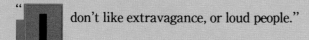 don't like extravagance, or loud people."

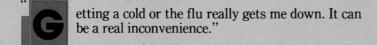 can't stand impatient people, even though I can get a bit impatient myself."

etting a cold or the flu really gets me down. It can be a real inconvenience."

ood is one of my real joys in life but one thing that I can't stomach is Alfalfa."

SURF'S UP

"I like to get in a car and go down the coast." Jason likes to get away from it all; he loves to surf at the beach resorts south west of Melbourne — Torquay, Apollo Bay, Anglesea and Lorne.

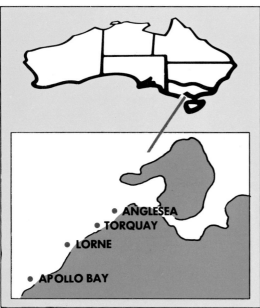

- ● ANGLESEA
- ● TORQUAY
- ● LORNE
- ● APOLLO BAY

Imagine. The sun in a blue sky that stretches to the horizon. The sand, yellow-white, warm, almost powdery beneath your feet. And the waves, blue-green rolling hills charging at the shore. You may as well be alone. Well, almost. For Jason, the hour and a half drive is soon forgotten. The Range Rover is parked and unpacked. Fifty yards away, the water beckons.

"You get this amazing mental and physical rush . . . it's like . . . there's nothing like coming down the face of a wave . . . the adrenalin feels incredible. To conquer something which is natural, where you've had to work at the way it's going instead of where you want to go. You're out in the sun, salt water. Salt water is God's gift, it's a cure for most things. For me, it cleans my skin. Mentally, it rejuvenates and relaxes. It's good fun."

Here, Jason can be himself. Just another surfer, not a celebrity. Other surfers may be there, but they too are bound up in the experience. Pressures are forgotten for simple pleasure.

"I water skied once and really enjoyed it. I like snow skiing too. But none of them compare to surfing. It's not the hassle of those other sports. You've got your board, you've got yourself; you don't need an engine, you don't need anything else. It's there. It's happening or it's not happening. And it's all natural."

Fetishes

"I like plain dishes, I'm not into very extravagant food."

Jason enjoys the quiet of breakfast most of all. At home he's likely to squeeze fresh orange juice and brew fresh coffee to go with his favourite cereal "Sustain".

At other times he is equally comfortable eating with friends at a restaurant or cooking at home. His favourites are Italian food, especially pasta dishes and veal dishes. "There's a really nice Italian restaurant, Cafe 'El Cucina, in Chapel street (in Melbourne), small, very authentic. Great food, great cappuccino." Other favourite foods include Japanese, and bread. Jason loves all types of bread; garlic bread, toast, and especially, Focaccia, an Italian style sandwich.

At home? "I don't get the opportunity much, but I love to cook. I think I have a knack for it. I always watched my step mother Marlene. She's a fantastic cook."

Imagine a cold, wet night. The soft sound of rain, windows with blurred wet trails. The fire crackles in the hearth and its glow fills the room. Dinner for two; soft music, quiet conversation. This is Jason's idea of a romantic evening, especially if he could cook something special and share it.

For Food

One of his favourites? Try this.

Veal Parmigiana

2 veal steaks, thinly sliced
1 tablespoon plain flour
1 egg
salt and pepper
2 tablespoons fresh breadcrumbs
oil for frying
1 oz butter
2 slices mozzarella cheese
Sauce
tablespoon of tomato paste
cup of diced skinless tomatoes
sprig of parsley
finely chopped onion
pinch of oregano
half oz. butter

Flatten the veal with rolling pin or meat mallet. Season with salt and pepper, dip into seasoned flour, then into beaten egg, then finally into breadcrumbs. Press with hand to firm the coating and chill on plate for 30 minutes.

Simmer onions in butter till golden, add tomatoes, paste and oregano and continue to simmer on very low. Add chopped parsley and a little water if necessary to maintain sauce texture.

Heat a little oil in a heavy frying pan. Add butter, when bubbling add veal. Cook until golden brown, turning twice during cooking. Place cheese slice on top of each. Serve when the cheese melts, spooning sauce over meat and cheese.

Great with scalloped potatoes and salad.

MY FAVOURITE MUSIC

"My taste in music has changed over the years. I used to like very alternative music, now I'm more into the mainstream. When I was younger, I liked stuff like New Order, The Cure, Heaven 17." He smiles as he remembers the days of sneaking into clubs while under-aged. Oddly enough, the opportunity to travel that has come with fame has exposed Jason to new influences. "The more and more I go to London, the more and more I begin to appreciate dance music."

So, what is Jason listening to? He says all types of music. "Like all music, you play a record so many times and you put it away; and you get another record and that becomes your favourite and so on." We asked him about particular favourites:

"KICK" *by INXS.*

"WHENEVER YOU NEED SOMEBODY" *by Rick Astley.*

"FAITH" *by George Michael.*

"SUBSTANCE" *by New Order.*

"BACK IN THE HIGH LIFE" *by Steve Winwood.*

"RATTLE AND HUM" *by U2.*

"NEW YORK" *by Lou Reed.*

"LOVE CHANGES EVERYTHING" *by Climie Fisher.*

Passion For Fashion

THE H

"THE HEROES is a fascinating action packed story about fourteen men who infiltrate behind enemy lines during World War II. It's based on a true story about some men who steal a small ship called the "Krait", and set out for Singapore. They spent three or four months disguised as Japanese, bared to the elements, without any back-up or support. It's a very courageous story. They managed to get through totally undetected and succeeded in sinking a lot of shipping."

S hooting THE HEROES took three months and Jason had to fit his scenes around his other commitments; NEIGHBOURS and his singing. This meant a very hectic schedule

for him; a few days here, a week there. The difficulty was that THE HEROES was largely shot in northern Queensland, around Cairns and Townsville, three thousand kilometres from Ramsay St.

For the small town of Cardwell, where several weeks were spent, the presence of seventy actors and film crew

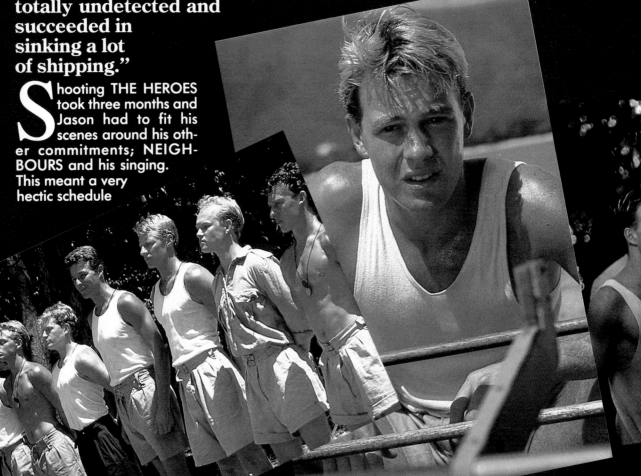

V. Mini Series
IEROES

created havoc. The locals were almost outnumbered. The presence of Jason, and several other well known television faces, created a stir. But the thoughts of one old local summed up the town's feeling: "I thought they'd be a bunch of bigheads, but they're great. Very quiet and well mannered, and they don't mind signing autographs for the kids."

Around here, the coast and the islands resemble the islands of Indonesia that the original Krait sailed through.

It was hard work but Jason enjoyed the challenge and the change of pace. He became quite attached to his part. "The character of "Happy" Housten is very unlike Scott, unlike any other character I've played." He threw himself into the work with true professionalism. "I felt it was a piece of history.

"Happy" was a very serious character, very strong minded, and close to his captain. He was vulnerable, because he was the youngest, a bit naive. All in all, a very interesting character."

Acting wasn't the only challenge. Many of the scenes were shot in mosquito infested swamps.

Jason recalls, "I got eaten alive . . . there was nothing I could do about them. I had to sit in the one position for ages to make sure it matched other shots."

For Jason, making this video was not only the most enjoyable so far, but will be the one to stay in his memory a long time. "I think it's a great video. I liked the set with its surfing theme, especially the sense of fun built into the approach."

The huge set was constructed at the biggest film studio in Australia. Tons of sand and an extraordinary series of painted backdrops were used to create the feel. Fifty extras were hired, their presence created a crowded, party atmosphere all night.

The concept was to create an early sixties surfing feel, and in that the production certainly succeeded. It's set around a surf lifesaving club where Jason "works". Here, he admires a girl from afar. Everything was carefully checked out, right down to the old surfing photographs, to ensure an authentic recreation.

It is meant to be a fun, slightly tongue-in-cheek atmosphere, and this comes through. Making it was a different story. It took twelve hours to shoot, beginning at four in the afternoon. By four in the morning, everyone was exhausted. Organising and amusing the extras during the long haul was a job in itself.

The next video, "Sealed with a kiss", continues the theme and story line, and was shot immediately afterwards. Of course, in the end, Jason gets the girl.

E R Y

THE VIDEO
Produced by:
Short Stories
Directed by:
Chris Langman
Location:
*Australian Film
Studios*

A

Y

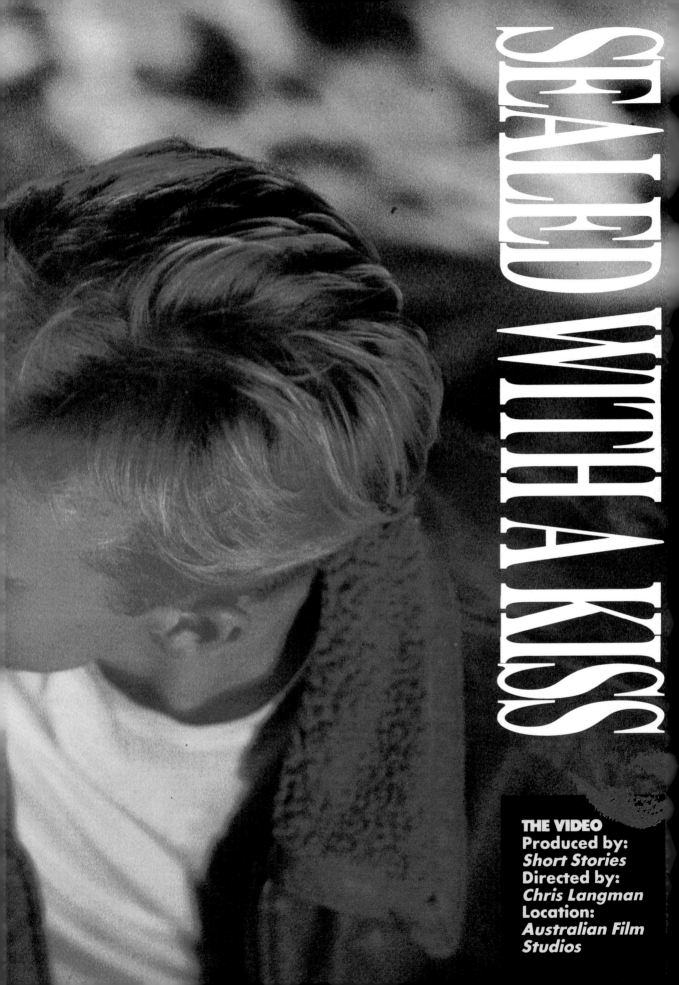

SEALED WITH A KISS

THE VIDEO
Produced by:
Short Stories
Directed by:
Chris Langman
Location:
Australian Film Studios

TEN
GOOD REASONS
THE ALBUM

"Basically, the recording of the album was done between January and March. I'd done "Nothing can divide us" last year, three songs in London early this year, and the rest was recorded in Australia. I think I've got more confident as time went on. Particularly with the last session when we recorded six songs, it took us five days."

Jason's father advised him to take piano lessons when he was a boy. In Australia, opportunities for straight dramatic actors are limited because of the small population. It was believed that music gave actors another dimension, a chance to make a living from musicals as well.

Neither of them could have foreseen the consequences for Jason. The album marks a new level in his entertainment career.

Everybody seems very pleased with it. The theme of the album is romance, about being in love. It touches something in all of us because we can all relate to those feelings.

The fac

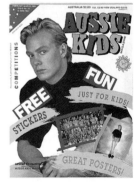

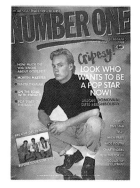

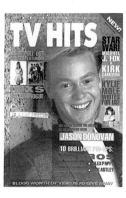

FUTURE
DIRECTIONS

"I never plan exactly what I'll do in the future because it hasn't happened that way for me in the past. But, at the same time, you've got to set yourself goals in order to achieve them. There are so many things to do, higher levels of achievement to reach for."

Jason is aware of the need to constantly improve and perfect his skills. He rates the ability to observe and learn from others and from experience as extremely important. He spends considerable time doing this himself; taking singing lessons and acting classes, continually striving to be better. He's not about to stand still and rest on his current achievements.

"I've done NEIGHBOURS for three and a half years and it's given me a lot of experience. It was a great training ground. Acting's in my blood I guess, and I'd really like to continue with that. At the moment, my recording is taking on a more international scale and I'm going to work on that. I'd love to do live concerts.

"I feel I can combine singing and acting. I'd like to do live work, and a film. I'm looking at one possibility later this year.

"My dream is to work in America. I went to New York and thought to myself, one day I'd like to make it here.

"I'm sure if I put my energies into learning and striving, the rest will come anyway. Of course you have to push yourself, promote yourself, to get into those situations. I can't imagine ever being bored. I guess we're lucky in the entertainment industry, your career can vary so much from one day to the next. If I was to do another film, my next move would be to do one that was bigger and better.

"It's the same with music. From one successful album, I could go on to the next, maybe write some songs for it or contribute to the production side of it."